CITY OF WATER TEOTIHUACAN CITY OF FIRE

A PICTORIAL

Fine Arts Museums of San Francisco • de Young

INTRODUCTION
TEOTIHUACAN: CITY OF THE GODS

Teotihuacan—the name of this archaeological site nestled in the northeastern part of the Valley of Mexico conjures visions of enormous pyramids and long avenues surrounded by mountains and volcanoes. But there is more to this place than meets the eye. Within and beneath the city's many plazas, buildings, and monumental structures lie secrets that are only now coming to light.

Established in the first century BCE, Teotihuacan evolved into a major urban center by the fifth century CE. Archeologists have determined that many groups of people migrated to Teotihuacan around 100 CE, although it is unclear what prompted these relocations. Occupying roughly eight square miles at its apogee, Teotihuacan was the largest and most densely populated city in the Western Hemisphere as well as the cultural, political, economic, and religious center of ancient Mesoamerica. Attracting a wide and diverse population of perhaps 100,000 people from throughout Mesoamerica, Teotihuacan integrated individuals of different backgrounds and traditions into the civic body through a citywide art and architectural program that promoted shared beliefs.

Three pyramids—two of immense proportions and a smaller third situated in a grand public square—anchor the center of the ancient city along the imposing boulevard known as the Street of the Dead. The city's main structures are all aligned on the same grid, oriented approximately fifteen degrees east of astronomical north—an arrangement that allowed the Moon Pyramid to be framed by the nearby peak Cerro Gordo. It is difficult to imagine

the sheer human effort it took to construct these grand architectural statements without the use of the wheel, draft animals, or metal tools.

A great fire around 550 CE marked Teotihuacan's downfall. There is evidence that the burning was intentional, as many ritual objects were also intentionally smashed and scattered at this time. Such acts were thought to divest these pieces of their ritual power. Teotihuacan's demise may have resulted from environmental difficulties or from political unrest and societal tensions rooted in the migrations into the Valley of Mexico. Whatever the cause, the systems of urban and religious maintenance devised by the city's leadership that had succeeded for over 400 years fell apart, and Teotihuacan's regional dominance ended.

To the Aztecs, who came to prominence almost 900 years after the fall of Teotihuacan, the ancient city was considered the place where the gods brought the world into existence. They gave it the name we use today, also naming the Sun and Moon Pyramids and the Street of the Dead. As they did in antiquity, Teotihuacan's scale and planning continue to inspire awe in visitors and scholars.

Teotihuacan: City of Water, City of Fire brings together artifacts from recent excavations with some found as long as a century ago. These finely crafted works of art demonstrate how the city's dominant ideology permeated everyday spaces, uniting a diverse population. Art provided a guide for citizens as they navigated Teotihuacan's streets and managed the natural resources within the Valley of Mexico. Water and fire were essential elements; they both powered and threatened the city through their presence or absence. The art of Teotihuacan represents, on a fundamental level, manifestations of these and other natural forces, and the beings and rituals designed to bring them into cosmic balance.

WHO WERE THE TEOTIHUACANOS?

In the first millennium BCE, people began settling in farming villages in the Teotihuacan Valley, southwest of where the city eventually developed. Although rainfall was not as high here as in areas to the south, these inhabitants were able to divert the courses of natural bodies of water to create an irrigated landscape favorable to the production of maize, beans, and squash—the primary diet of Mesoamericans—and, consequently, the growth of a civilization.

Tens of thousands of new migrants came to the area in the first centuries CE, although the reasons for this demographic surge are still mysterious. Scholars ascribe it to a combination of volcanic eruptions to the south, which caused a northward migration to Teotihuacan, and the city's growing appeal as an economic hub, a sacred place, and a powerful capital. The construction of the Moon Pyramid early in the city's history suggests that its importance as a religious site may have attracted people to Teotihuacan and led to the foundation of its early government.

The city became a large, cosmopolitan place where migrant communities spoke multiple languages and lived in ethnic enclaves—comparable in many ways to modern cities. Most of Teotihuacan's citizens lived comfortably in multifamily apartment compounds organized around neighborhood centers. Although there was a socioeconomic hierarchy, citizens lived more equally here than in many other ancient cities. Yet they worked without benefit of wheeled vehicles or work animals; people performed all of the labor required to build and maintain the city, develop its extensive trade networks, and extract and import raw materials. As in most early, densely settled cities, disease also took its toll.

Civic leaders were certainly powerful, but they did not use the art of Teotihuacan to name or promote themselves. Rather, these leaders fostered a collective identity and ideology that united the multiethnic population. The state religious system encouraged shared interests in agricultural fertility; appeasement of the gods to continue cycles of time and maintain the cosmic order; and preservation of military might, which kept trade routes open for the movement of goods, keeping the economy robust, and also allowed Teotihuacan to thrive without the need for fortifications. All of these themes are expressed in the art and architecture of Teotihuacan.

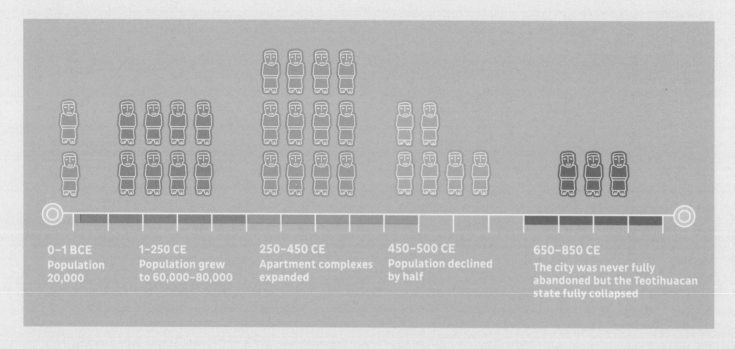

0–1 BCE
Population 20,000

1–250 CE
Population grew to 60,000–80,000

250–450 CE
Apartment complexes expanded

450–500 CE
Population declined by half

650–850 CE
The city was never fully abandoned but the Teotihuacan state fully collapsed

TEOTIHUACAN AND RELIGION

Teotihuacan religious practices promoted a sense of shared identity among a diverse population. For all segments of Teotihuacan society, religion permeated daily life. While the pyramids and plazas were sites for spectacular ritual events, small household shrines throughout the city were dedicated to a variety of lesser domestic deities.

THE STORM GOD

The patron deity of Teotihuacan was the Storm God. As a being of enormous powers, the Storm God had the ability to create lightning, make fire, and wreak destruction. He is also associated with war. Among his identifying elements are arching eyebrows or "goggled" eyes, a curved upper lip, and prominent fangs. He sometimes holds a lightning scepter. The Storm God was depicted in many different guises, characterized by distinct colors and attributes. Other representations depict elite figures impersonating the Storm God, such as the goggle-eyed figure on this vessel.

THE MAIZE GOD

The cultivation of maize is one of the defining characteristics of Mesoamerican culture, yet there is no readily identifiable Maize God in Teotihuacan. Scholars propose that representations of a youthful male—a physical and cultural ideal—typically rendered in greenstone or jade, colors associated with maize, may represent the Maize God. About three dozen masks that fit this description have been found throughout Teotihuacan; hundreds of others can be seen in museums around the world.

FEATHERED SERPENT

The Feathered Serpent—the supreme creator of time and space—was the ultimate symbol of power and warfare. It was under the auspices of this deity that the rulers of Teotihuacan claimed their political authority. The Feathered Serpent is represented by a large snake swimming across the primordial waters, typically covered by the characteristic green iridescent feathers of the quetzal bird. It often appears as part of military insignia and regalia.

TRIPOD VESSEL WITH GOGGLE-EYED FIGURE

450–550. Ceramic with post-fire stucco and pigments, 5 5/8 × 5 7/8 in. (14.3 ×14.9 cm). Los Angeles County Museum of Art, Gift of Constance McCormick Fearing, AC1993.217.16

MASK

300–600. Green serpentine, 8 1/2 × 8 1/16 × 4 1/8 in. (21.6 × 20.5 × 10.5 cm). Dumbarton Oaks Research Library and Collection, Robert Woods Bliss Collection, PC.B.054

BATON (DETAIL)

70–80. Wood, 21 7/8 × 3 1/4 × 3/4 in. (55.6 × 8.2 × 2 cm). Zona de Monumentos Arqueológicos de Teotihuacán / INAH, 10-411013

THE FEATHERED SERPENT PYRAMID, CIUDADELA, AND TUNNEL

The Feathered Serpent Pyramid takes its name from the undulating serpents carved into its sides. Although it is the smallest of the three pyramids that dominate the center of Teotihuacan, its elaborate decoration marks its significance: all four facades were covered in monumental carvings of these creatures, their heads surrounded by wreaths of feathers. The serpents' bodies support facelike headdresses with nose pendants. These symbols may represent a Primordial Crocodile, a sign later used by the Aztecs to signal the beginning of a new era. They may also represent a specific kind of headdress associated with rulership and warfare. The carved shells surrounding the serpents' bodies express the importance of water, which is further expressed by the iconography of the surrounding architecture.

Excavations have identified a series of large-scale sacrificial offerings apparently dedicated at the time of the pyramid's construction, around 250 CE. Tombs containing more than 137 warrior-priests sacrificed and buried with abundant offerings were found in the interior and exterior of the pyramid. The symbolism of the Feathered Serpent deity expresses warfare and the preeminent power of the leaders who directed the site's construction. The proclamation of the divine authority of the rulers was captured not only in the monumental architecture but also in the massive burials that must have taken years to prepare and finally integrate into the construction. The site seems to have been a sacred precinct of considerable importance for the state.

The Feathered Serpent Pyramid is enclosed in an enormous plaza known as the Ciudadela ("Citadel"), a place for Teotihuacanos to gather and engage in large public rituals. The complex has a larger footprint than that of the city's biggest structure, the Sun Pyramid. Archaeological evidence suggests that this immense plaza may have been periodically flooded in rituals that turned it into a simulacrum of the primordial sea of Mesoamerican creation myth. The Feathered Serpent Pyramid thus symbolically became the sacred mountain that, in this narrative, emerged from the primordial sea at the dawn of time. Time and the ancient Mesoamerican calendar were cyclical and required renewal through ceremony. The Ciudadela may have been the site of massive ceremonies held to appease the gods and also to remind Teotihuacan's populace of the leaders' divine right to exercise authority under the auspices of the Feathered Serpent.

EFFIGY VESSEL
100–200. Ceramic, 6 ¼ × 9 ⅝ × 5 in. (16 × 24.5 × 12.7 cm).
Zona de Monumentos Arqueológicos de Teotihuacán / INAH

Feathered Serpent Pyramid at Teotihuacan

TLALOCAN (THE TUNNEL)

In 2003, Mexican archaeologists discovered a tunnel running 113 yards from the center of the Ciudadela east to a position directly beneath the Feathered Serpent Pyramid. Further research indicated this tunnel was made early in Teotihuacan's history, around 100 CE, before the pyramid's construction. Investigation and interpretation of the site and these finds is ongoing, but more than a decade later, scholars have established that the tunnel was manmade and that it was apparently sealed and re-entered on multiple occasions between the time it was first built and its permanent closure (around 250 CE, which coincides with the construction of the Feathered Serpent Pyramid).

In Mesoamerican cosmology, the "sacred cave" found beneath the primordial mountain represented the entrance and path to the underworld, an aquatic place filled with riches and nourishing seeds, and inhabited by deities responsible for maintaining order in the universe. If the Feathered Serpent Pyramid is a stand-in for the sacred mountain, then the tunnel beneath it may represent this watery underworld and was perhaps the most important ritual space in Teotihuacan. This theory is supported by many of the discoveries: For example, the tunnel itself had been dug to the level of the water table, providing ancient Teotihuacanos with access to the spring water that comes from the depths of the earth. The walls of the tunnel itself had been embedded by its builders with a reflective mineral, pyrite, to produce a magical, sparkling effect.

More than 50,000 objects were deposited as offerings in the tunnel. Near the tunnel's final chamber, directly beneath the center of the Feathered Serpent Pyramid, is an offering believed to mark the *axis mundi*—a symbolic pillar connecting heaven, earth, and underworld as well as the juncture of the four cardinal directions. This offering contained four enigmatic sculptures, some apparently carrying bags of greenstone objects and iron-ore mirrors and discs. These figures suggest a deeper, more ritual significance and may represent Teotihuacan's founding ancestors, witnesses to the birth of time.

Two standing anthropomorphic sculptures discovered in the tunnel beneath the pyramid near the point where the *axis mundi* was located

STANDING FIGURE
200–250. Greenstone, 18 1/2 × 7 1/2 in. (47 × 19 cm). Zona de Monumentos Arqueológicos de Teotihuacán / INAH

STANDING FIGURE
200–250. Greenstone, 14 1/8 × 6 1/2 in. (36 × 16.5 cm). Zona de Monumentos Arqueológicos de Teotihuacán / INAH

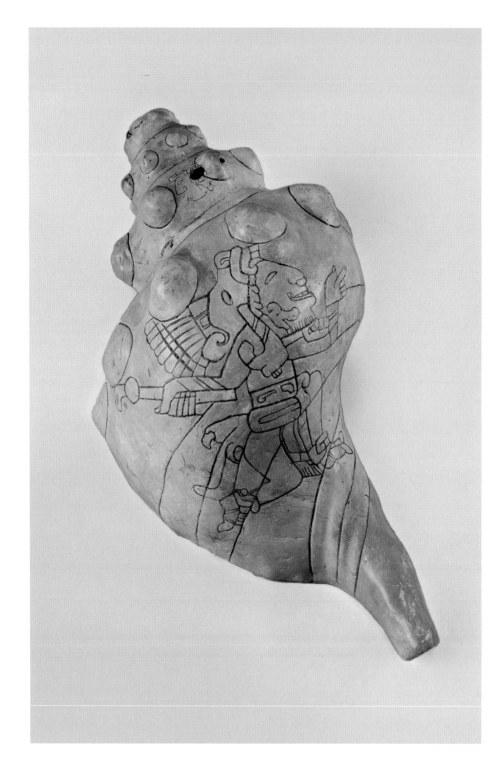

INCISED SHELL

150–250. Shell, 15 ³/₈ × 8 ¹/₄ in. (39 × 21 cm). Zona de Monumentos Arqueológicos de Teotihuacán / INAH

PENDANT WITH AVIAN MOTIFS
200–250. Shell. 2½ × 1½ in. (6.4 × 3.9 cm). Zona de
Monumentos Arqueológicos de Teotihuacán / INAH

STORM GOD VESSEL
150–250. Ceramic, 11 1/4 × 8 1/4 in. (28.5 × 21 cm). Zona de
Monumentos Arqueológicos de Teotihuacán / INAH

TRIPOD VESSEL
200–250. Ceramic and mineral pigments, 6 1/4 × 6 7/8 in.
(15.8 × 17.4 cm). Zona de Monumentos Arqueológicos de
Teotihuacán / INAH

STORM GOD DISK

350–550. Ceramic, 7½ × 1⅛ in. (19 × 3 cm). Zona de
Monumentos Arqueológicos de Teotihuacán / INAH

EFFIGY BUNDLE

400–550. Ceramic, 12 ⁵⁄₈ × 6 ¾ × 9 in. (32 × 17 × 23 cm).
Zona de Monumentos Arqueológicos de Teotihuacán /
INAH, 10-336692 0/2

MASK

150–250. Greenstone and pyrite, 4 1/4 × 4 3/8 × 2 7/8 in.
(10.8 × 11.2 × 7.4 cm). Zona de Monumentos Arqueológicos
de Teotihuacán / INAH, 10-615838

THE SUN PYRAMID

The Sun Pyramid dominates the center of the city. It is Teotihuacan's most massive monument, and one of the largest ever built in the ancient world. The structure was built in one single, massive effort around 200 CE, resulting in a building with four tiers (its current appearance, with five tiers and an *adosada*, or attached frontal platform, is the result of a misguided attempt at reconstruction early in the twentieth century). Its square plan covers roughly 60,000 square yards, and it rises 200 feet high, making it one of the tallest buildings in the Western Hemisphere until the advent of the modern skyscraper.

This pyramid was probably Teotihuacan's first great monumental construction effort and established a clear epicenter for the city. Its prominence suggests that it was associated with a powerful religious cult, perhaps one that legitimized the political power of its leadership. Various investigations over the last century have revealed many details about its construction. The most recent project has identified offerings dated to the building's earliest phases, as well as evidence for exterior sculptural programs depicting motifs related to fire and jaguars. The symbolic importance of the Sun Pyramid connects it with the calendar, governmental power, and the element of fire. Sculptures found around the structure suggest that this was a place where rituals were performed—perhaps similar to the Aztec New Fire ceremony—that related to renewal of time and of the ruling elite's authority.

But the Sun Pyramid also serves to demonstrate how Teotihuacanos did not construct even their most impressive buildings in isolation; instead it was part of a larger architectural program designed to describe a specific worldview in material form. This pyramid combined with the Moon Pyramid to symbolize a complementary duality: the Sun Pyramid probably represented fire, warmth, the dry season, masculinity, and the sun, whereas the Moon Pyramid symbolized water, the rainy season, land, fertility, femininity, and the moon.

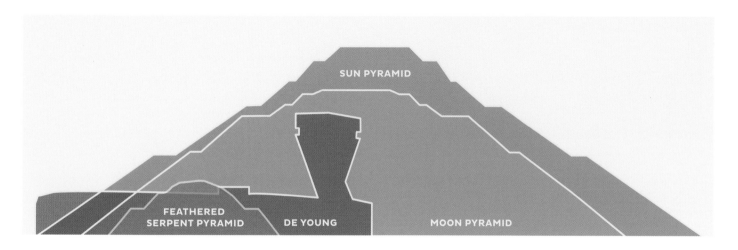

SYMBOLS AT THE SUN PYRAMID

OLD FIRE GOD

Archaeologists believe that the Sun Pyramid supported a temple on its summit, which may have housed a large stone carving of an elderly, cross-legged figure burdened by a large circular brazier that presses down on his head and neck. This represents the Old Fire God. He is associated with fire and volcanoes, and sculptures of this god are frequently made from volcanic rock. Fire was an essential force that both powered and threatened the city; it required careful management and appeasement of the deity who controlled it. Images of the Old Fire God played an important role in unifying the city. Earlier versions of this deity appeared in central and western Mexico. More than one hundred Old Fire God figures have been found throughout Teotihuacan, signifying its importance to a diverse migrant population.

THE FELINES OF TEOTIHUACAN

Aggressive and fearsome, felines were seen as beings with superhuman powers and were regarded as protectors of warriors and priests. These creatures are seen throughout the city but are especially represented in the northeastern district of Teotihuacan, dominated by the Sun Pyramid. Sculptural representations of felines that have been discovered there include fourteen heads and eleven forearms and claws. The pyramid's decoration also included felines eating human hearts. This image possibly refers to warfare and sacrifice, and to the participation of carnivores in sacrificial rituals.

OLD FIRE GOD SCULPTURE
500–600. Andesite, 24 × 26 × 19 ¾ in. (61 × 66 × 50 cm).
Zona de Monumentos Arqueológicos de Teotihuacán / INAH

FELINE SCULPTURE
300–400. Andesite and pigments, 22 ⅞ × 20 ½ × 48 ⅞ in.
(58 × 52 × 124 cm). Zona de Monumentos Arqueológicos de
Teotihuacán / INAH, 10-411215

RATTLESNAKE TAIL SCULPTURE

300–400. Andesite, 41 × 31 × 15 in. (106 × 80 × 38.1 cm).
Zona de Monumentos Arqueológicos de Teotihuacán / INAH,
10-412426

STORM GOD *ALMENA* (BUILDING MARKER)

350–550, Ceramic, 22⅞ × 15½ in. (58 × 39.5 cm). Museo Nacional de Antropología / INAH, 10-213194

FELINE *ALMENA* (BUILDING MARKER)
350–550. *Tecali* (onyx), 11 × 13 ⅝ × 2 ⅝ × in. (28 × 34.5 × 6.6
cm). Museo Nacional de Antropología / INAH, 10-80885

THE MOON PYRAMID

A modest temple constructed at the very beginning of Teotihuacan's history, at around 50 to 100 CE, suggests the presence of a powerful religion, which may have attracted many of the migrants from the surrounding areas at this early date. Over the centuries, this temple was enlarged several times into what is now the massive Moon Pyramid. It is the second-largest monument at Teotihuacan, with a rectangular base covering about 30,000 square yards and four main tiers reaching a height of approximately 141 feet.

The most significant of the pyramid's expansions, around 250 CE, indicates a period of increasing wealth and political centralization in the city. Elaborate buried offerings were made at the dedication of this larger pyramid. Placed in each burial were carefully arranged groups of greenstone and obsidian sculptures, slate, pyrite, and ceramic objects. Human and animal skeletons were also found in many of the Moon Pyramid burials. The burials and offerings record complex rituals apparently timed to different phases of the building's construction. As a whole, those that contained abundant offerings of exceptional quality were apparently not dedicated to a single individual or a particular deity, but rather were fundamentally representations of Teotihuacan cosmic ideology, evoking supreme authority, militarism, and human and animal sacrifice. Intriguingly, there is little evidence to suggest an exterior sculptural program for the building itself, though monumental sculptures may have been located on and around the pyramid and on the platforms that surround its central plaza. These smaller buildings also provided access to complexes including the so-called Quetzalpapalotl Palace.

Excavations of obsidian workshops near the Moon Pyramid suggest a certain degree of state control over the production and distribution of specific forms of weaponry and ritual items. Eighteen obsidian eccentrics were found in one offering, a number that is associated with marking time on the calendar. These curving blades, some with serrated edges, resemble the lightning bolts held by the Storm God.

One of the most noteworthy factors in the set of Moon Pyramid dedicatory burials was the emphasis on femininity. A greenstone female figure standing on a large pyrite disk and facing west was found exactly at the center of the entire complex. Femininity, water, and fertility formed symbolic connections at the Moon Pyramid, making a possible association of the pyramid with the moon and rain.

MOSAIC FIGURE

200–250. Serpentine, greenstone, and shell, 10 × 4 1/8 × 1 7/8 in. (25.4 × 10.6 × 4.8 cm). Zona de Monumentos Arqueológicos de Teotihuacán / INAH, 10-615743

Moon Pyramid at Teotihuacan

MATERIALS AND MEANING

OBSIDIAN: UTILITY AND RITUAL

Obsidian is the glass that results from the violent heating and eventual cooling of volcanic lava. When flaked it produces an extremely sharp edge, and it has been used for thousands of years as a cutting tool. As a highly valuable trade commodity, obsidian played a crucial role in the establishment of the Teotihuacan state. The early leaders figured out how to gain control over obsidian deposits outside of the city, organize work crews to acquire the raw material, and bring it back to Teotihuacan. They also oversaw the artisans who carved it into utilitarian blades and elaborate ritual figures.

THE POWER OF GREEN

Jade and greenstone were extremely valuable materials for the ancient Teotihuacanos. Many of these precious stones came from afar, imported along Teotihuacan's vast supply and trade networks. They were prized for their green color, which served to symbolically represent maize and agricultural fertility. Early Teotihuacanos were able to efficiently farm maize by rerouting water sources and developing complex irrigation systems to produce a supply of food adequate for a large population. The success of the maize crop was crucial to ensuring the survival of the city.

STANDING FIGURE
200–250. Red obsidian, 10 × 3 × ¾ in. (25.3 × 7.5 × 1.9 cm).
Zona de Monumentos Arqueológicos de Teotihuacán / INAH

STANDING FIGURE WITH EARFLARES
200–250. Greenstone, pyrite, and shell. 12 × 4½ × 3 in.
(30.6 × 11.4 × 7.6 cm). Zona de Monumentos Arqueológicos
de Teotihuacán / INAH

SHELL: COASTAL CONNECTIONS

The availability of shells originating from both the Gulf and Pacific Coasts demonstrates Teotihuacan's far-reaching channels of contact and exchange. Marine shells were fertility symbols and also represented the watery underworld of creation. Such associations were reinforced not only through the use of shell as a physical material but also by representations of shells in murals, for example. Shells formed a frequent component of burials at all three pyramids, both as objects and as the raw material for necklaces such as this example, made of more than three hundred individual pieces of shell carved to look like human teeth.

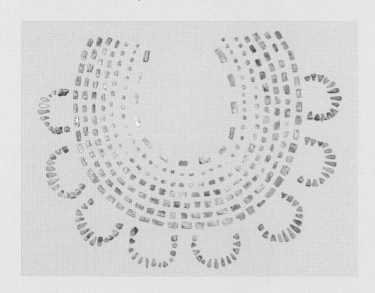

TECALI: POWER AND PRESTIGE

Tecali is the name applied to a greenish-white stone that is also known variously as Mexican onyx, travertine, alabaster, or onyx marble. Teotihuacanos obtained *tecali* from quarries in what is now the state of Puebla. The name derives from the district there called Tecali (in Nahuatl, the language of the Aztecs, "houses of stone"). The material appears to have been highly valued for its translucent qualities. A number of feline figures in *tecali*, such as this effigy from the Quetzalpapalotl Palace near the Moon Pyramid, have been found at Teotihuacan.

NECKLACE
200–250. Shell, 18 ¾ × 24 ⅞ × ⅜ in. (47.6 × 63.3 × 1 cm)
(as mounted). Zona de Monumentos Arqueológicos de
Teotihuacán / INAH, 10–615828 0/352

FELINE EFFIGY
400–550. Tecali, 7 ¾ × 5 ¼ × 6 ¼ in. (19.6 × 13.4 × 15.7 cm).
Museo Nacional de Antropología / INAH, 10–78331

ECCENTRIC
200–250. Obsidian, 2 ⁵/₈ × 15 ¹/₈ × ⁵/₈ in. (6.7 × 38.4 × 1.6 cm).
Zona de Monumentos Arqueológicos de Teotihuacán / INAH,
10–615741

SEATED FIGURINE
250–300. Greenstone, 2 ³/₈ × 1 ³/₈ × 1 in. (6.1 × 3.5 × 2.6 cm).
Zona de Monumentos Arqueológicos de Teotihuacán / INAH,
10-615747 1/2

PENDANT
200–250. Shell, 4 ¼ × 2 ⅝ × ⅛ in. (10.8 × 6.7 × 0.2 cm).
Zona de Monumentos Arqueológicos de Teotihuacán / INAH,
10-615744

AVIAN *ALMENA* (BUILDING MARKER)
200–600. Ceramic, 17 ¾ × 18 ½ × 1 in. (45.1 × 47 × 2.5 cm).
Museo Nacional de Antropología / INAH, 10-80855

APARTMENTS AND BARRIOS

Outside of the ceremonial core of the city, consisting of the three major pyramids, the Street of the Dead, and administrative centers such as the Quetzalpapalotl Palace and Xalla, a large portion of Teotihuacan was made up of architecturally similar residential complexes in areas such as Tlajinga, the Oaxaca Barrio, Tetitla, La Ventilla, and Techinantitla. These were built in a gridlike layout that conformed to the overall plan of the city. These apartments were occupied by extended family groups often specializing in specific craft production such as obsidian or ceramics. It is estimated that there were around two thousand apartment compounds throughout Teotihuacan, ranging in physical size and level of decoration. In many cases the walls were decorated with mural paintings, most elaborately in the administrative centers and the dwellings of the upper and middle classes.

Teotihuacan was a center of commerce and production that extended far beyond its borders. Its trading network was vast, reaching both the Atlantic and the Pacific Oceans. Archaeologists believe that the residents of certain neighborhoods served as communities that managed trade. The richly colored paintings of Tetitla, for example, along with the abundant presence of shells as offerings and as an artistic subject, indicate that although the compound itself was of fairly typical size, Tetitla's residents were high-status shell traders with ties to other parts of Mesoamerica, particularly the Maya region.

Although we do not know the dominant language spoken by Teotihuacanos, we do know that the city was home to a variety of ethnic groups from different parts of Mesoamerica who spoke multiple languages. Some resided in ethnic enclaves, where they carried out some of the cultural practices of their homelands at the same time they integrated themselves into the cultural fabric of the city. Artifacts found in all parts of the city suggest that traditions from other regions thrived alongside Teotihuacan styles. Many of the migrants also seemed to specialize in trade. In the northeastern Merchants' Barrio, for example, a group with ties to north-central Veracruz imported valuable materials such as ceramics, jade, amber, flint, and seashells.

FELINE HEAD

200–350. Ceramic, 6 ⁷/₈ × 8 ¹/₂ × 5 ¹/₄ in. (17.5 × 21.7 × 13.5 cm). Zona de Monumentos Arqueológicos de Teotihuacán / INAH, 10–615789

La Ventilla at Teotihuacan

MURALS

Teotihuacan's residential compounds typically held a number of family apartments around a common courtyard. In many cases the walls of these shared spaces were decorated with elaborate mural paintings. These were painted directly into the walls' wet plaster, creating an extremely durable surface. As the upper walls crumbled over time, only the paintings on the lower registers have survived. The murals' imagery mirrored that of the larger building programs, creating a common visual vocabulary throughout the city.

This Feathered Serpent mural from an apartment compound illustrates how residential imagery often reinforced larger building programs and civic ideology. Like this mural, the Feathered Serpent Pyramid's facade was originally colored with green and red pigment. The red background represents the sacred cosmic realms of the upper and underworld. Sparkling hematite and pyrite were mixed into the paint, creating a shimmering surface that would have been activated by light reflected from shallow pools in the compound's central patio. As in the sparkling tunnel beneath the pyramid, these perceptual effects would have re-created the environment of the watery underworld.

**FEATHERED SERPENTS
AND FLOWERING TREES MURAL
(FEATHERED SERPENT 1)**

500–550. Earthen aggregate, stucco, and mineral pigments,
22¼ × 160¼ in. (56.5 × 407 cm). Fine Arts Museums of San
Francisco, Bequest of Harald J. Wagner, 1985.104.1a–d

EFFIGY JAR

350–550, Ceramic, 5 ⁷⁄₈ × 5 ¹⁄₈ in. (14.8 × 13 cm). Zona de
Monumentos Arqueológicos de Teotihuacán / INAH

AVIAN EFFIGY VESSEL

250–350. Ceramic, shell, greenstone, and stucco, 9 ¹⁄₈ ×
9 ¹⁄₂ × 13 ¾ in. (23.2 × 24 × 35 cm). Museo Nacional de
Antropología / INAH, 10-80489

**MURAL FRAGMENT
(BIRD WITH SHIELD AND SPEAR)**

500–550. Earthen aggregate, lime plaster, and mineral
pigments. 11 5/8 × 12 3/8 in. (29.5 × 31.5 cm). Fine Arts
Museums of San Francisco, Bequest of Harald J. Wagner,
1985.104.9

***INCENSARIO* (INCENSE BURNER)**

350–450. Ceramic, mica, and mineral pigments. 26 1/2 ×
17 3/8 × 9 1/2 in. (67.4 × 44 × 24 cm). Zona de Monumentos
Arqueológicos de Teotihuacán / INAH, 10–412410 0/2

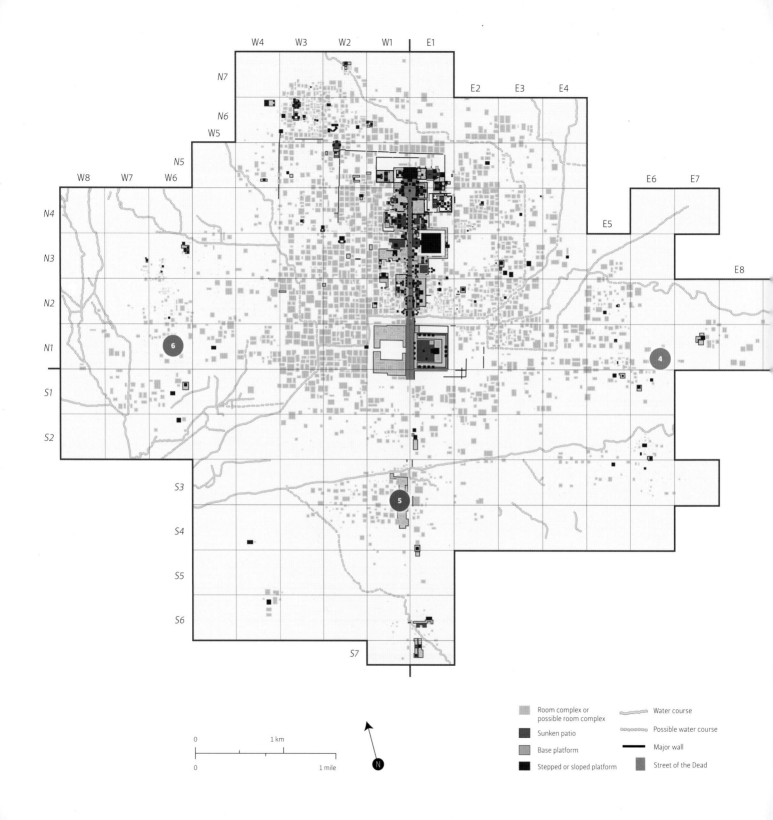

W4	W3	W2	W1	E1					

N7

N6

W5

N5

W8   W7   W6

E2   E3   E4

E6   E7

N4

E5

N3

E8

N2

N1   ⑥   ④

S1

S2

S3   ⑤

S4

S5

S6

S7

0   1 km

0   1 mile

N

	Room complex or possible room complex		Water course
	Sunken patio		Possible water course
	Base platform		Major wall
	Stepped or sloped platform		Street of the Dead

MAP OF TEOTIHUACAN

1. FEATHERED SERPENT PYRAMID, TUNNEL, CIUDADELA

2. SUN PYRAMID

3. MOON PYRAMID

4. EAST PLATFORM

5. TLAJINGA

6. OAXACA BARRIO

7. TETITLA

8. LA VENTILLA

9. STREET OF THE DEAD COMPLEX

10. TECHINANTITLA

11. XALLA

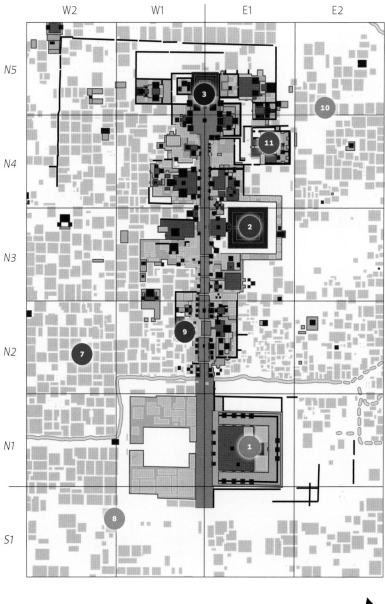

DETAIL OF TEOTIHUACAN'S CORE

Published by the Fine Arts Museums of San Francisco
on the occasion of the exhibition
Teotihuacan: City of Water, City of Fire.

de Young
September 30, 2017–February 11, 2018

Los Angeles County Museum of Art
March 25–July 15, 2018

This exhibition is organized by the Fine Arts Museums of
San Francisco and the Los Angeles County Museum of Art,
in collaboration with the Secretaría de Cultura through the
Instituto Nacional de Antropología e Historia de México.

This exhibition has been made possible in part by a major
grant from the National Endowment for the Humanities:
Exploring the human endeavor.

Presenting Sponsors
Diane B. Wilsey
The Donald L. Wyler Trust

Conservator's Circle
The Charles D. and Frances K. Field Fund

Benefactor's Circle
Douglas A. Tilden
Wells Fargo

Patron's Circle
Janet Barnes and Thomas W. Weisel Family
Walter and Elise Haas Fund
The Selz Foundation, Inc.

Additional support is provided by Carol and Lyman Casey,
and Alec and Gail Merriam.

Any views, findings, conclusions, or recommendations
expressed in this exhibition do not necessarily represent
those of the National Endowment for the Humanities.

Portions of this book were adapted from the exhibition
catalogue *Teotihuacan: City of Water, City of Fire*, edited by
Matthew H. Robb (San Francisco: Fine Arts Museums of San
Francisco; and Oakland: University of California Press, 2017).

Published by the
Fine Arts Museums of San Francisco
Golden Gate Park
50 Hagiwara Tea Garden Drive
San Francisco, CA 94118
www.famsf.org

Max Hollein, Director and CEO
Sheila Pressley, Director of Education

Leslie Dutcher, Director of Publications
Danica Michels Hodge, Managing Editor
Jane Hyun, Editor
Diana K. Murphy, Editorial Assistant

Edited by Danica Michels Hodge
Designed and typeset by Bob Aufuldish, Aufuldish & Warinner
Printing and binding by Susan Willis, Willis Print Network, at
Dome Printing, Sacramento